GROUP CURRICU...

# THE
# *Love Dare*

## FOR PARENTS

## BIBLE STUDY

STEPHEN KENDRICK
ALEX KENDRICK
As developed with TRAVIS AGNEW

B&H Publishing Group • Nashville, Tennessee

Published by LifeWay Press®
© 2013 Stephen and Alex Kendrick

ISBN 9781430028918 • Item 005602392

Dewey decimal classification: 649
Subject headings: PARENTING \ PARENT-CHILD RELATIONSHIP \ BIBLE–STUDY

Scripture quotations are taken from the Holman Christian Standard Bible®, copyright © 1999,
2000, 2002, 2003 by Holman Bible Publishers. Used by permission.

Scripture quotations marked NASB are taken from the New American Standard Bible®, Copyright
© 1960, 1962, 1963, 1968, 1971, 1972, 1973, 1975, 1977, 1995 by The Lockman Foundation. Used
by permission. (www.lockman.org)

To order additional copies of this resource: write LifeWay Church Resources Customer Service;
One LifeWay Plaza; Nashville, TN 37234-0113; fax 615.251.5933; phone 800.458.2772;
email orderentry@lifeway.com; order online at www.lifeway.com; or visit the LifeWay Christian Store
serving you.

Printed in the United States of America

Adult Ministry Publishing
LifeWay Church Resources
One LifeWay Plaza
Nashville, TN 37234-0152

# Contents

# ABOUT THE AUTHORS

**STEPHEN KENDRICK** serves as senior associate pastor of preaching and prayer at Sherwood Church, in Albany, Georgia (*sherwoodbaptist.net*). He has served as co-writer and producer of Sherwood Pictures' movies. Stephen and his brother, Alex, co-wrote COURAGEOUS curriculum *Honor Begins at Home* and *Courageous Living Bible Study*. FIREPROOF resources include *The Love Dare Bible Study* and the *New York Times* bestseller *The Love Dare*.

Before joining Sherwood in 2001, Stephen served as a youth minister in Atlanta. He and his wife, Jill, live in Albany with their four children. One of Stephen's greatest joys is watching his kids continue to grow in wisdom, stature, and in favor with God and man.

**ALEX KENDRICK** has served as associate pastor of movie outreach at Sherwood Church and co-writer and director of Sherwood's movies. In addition, he is a speaker, author, and actor—filling the roles of Grant Taylor in FACING THE GIANTS and Adam Mitchell in COURAGEOUS.

Before attending New Orleans Baptist Theological Seminary, Alex was a Christian disc jockey for two radio stations and a minister to college students in Marietta, Georgia. He and his wife, Christina, have six children and live in Albany. His proudest moments involve seeing his children make godly decisions and grow in Christian character.

**TRAVIS AGNEW** worked alongside Stephen and Alex to develop *The Love Dare for Parents Bible Study*. His passion is to disciple people through preaching, teaching, writing, and worship. Travis has recorded worship projects, authored books, and frequently blogs about fatherhood, family, and faith (*travisagnew.org*). Married to Amanda, he is the proud father of two sons and one daughter. Travis is the worship pastor at North Side Baptist Church in Greenwood, South Carolina.

## ABOUT THIS STUDY

The purpose of *The Love Dare for Parents Bible Study* is to equip parents to be all that God intended them to be by addressing key issues related to loving and training up strong, godly children. Parents will find scriptural support for how God has blessed them with children, for being a godly role model, for relating to each child based on his or her uniqueness, for preparing kids for life's difficulties, and for launching them well to start their own families and carry on a strong legacy for future generations.

Group sessions are designed for a minimum of one hour each week; feel free to add more interaction and discussion as your schedule allows. Your resources include this workbook, your group facilitator, and *The Love Dare for Parents* (encouraged, but optional). Be willing to participate with your group by sharing about yourself and your family, engaging in group discussions, and expressing your own joys and concerns about parenting.

**REFLECT**, **RETHINK**, and **RENEW** are the three basic elements of each group discussion. **REFLECT** starts the group process by helping parents get acquainted and identify some aspect of their family roles or experiences. **RETHINK** points the group to some aspect of God's plan for the home—and redirects the group for any new ways of thinking that might be insightful or helpful. **RENEW** offers application, done either during the group time or at home between sessions.

Those who include reading and doing *The Love Dare for Parents* with their Bible study will have rich parenting insights to share with their group. (See pp. 86-87 for an overview.)

# GROUP GUIDELINES

*When parents know that others are supporting, encouraging, and*
*praying for them, it encourages them on their journey with God.*
*No one is able to walk this parenting path alone. It is vital to*
*covenant together and agree on principles that guide your group*
*process, launching you into growth and Christian community.*

## SEVEN COMMITMENTS FOR GROUP SUCCESS

**Priority:** We will give high priority to group meetings and to the commitments we need to make to our families, especially as we parent our children.

**Preparation and Participation:** We will participate without dominating. We will strive to come to group having read through the study material, ready to discuss it.

**Respect:** Our group will provide a safe place to share our hearts openly without fear of judgment or ridicule. Scripture teaches us to be quick to listen and slow to speak (Jas. 1:19). We will speak the truth in love (Eph. 4:15) and value one another's opinions, while allowing the Scripture to help us come to godly conclusions.

**Confidentiality:** In sharing thoughts and feelings related to our home, marriage, and relationship with God, we will keep all information in the strictest confidence. What happens in group time stays in group time. However, no one will be required to share.

**Life Change:** In each session we will identify aspects that need attention in our walk as a believer, parent, spouse, and friend.

**Care and Support:** We agree to provide care and encouragement for every member, praying for each other. (Some group members may also want to enlist support from prayer warriors not in the study, *being careful not to give anything shared in confidence.*)

**Accountability:** We agree to let the members of the group hold us accountable to the commitments we make in whatever loving ways we mutually decide. As a group, we choose to commit to the accountability that is necessary to stay the course.

*When parents unconditionally love their children and children delight in their parents, the world gets a glimpse of the gospel: a Heavenly Father's deep love for His Son in whom He is well pleased and a loyal Son's deep love for, honor toward, and delight in His Father.*

*The more that this incredible dynamic is modeled and experienced in our homes, the more it powerfully attracts the people of this world to the gospel and to the heart of our Heavenly Father and to His Son. It awakens in our hearts the desire to know this loving God intimately (John 17:20-24).*

Signed,

_____

Date: _____

## SESSION 1

# Sacred Trust

Children are a blessing
and a gift from God.

## REFLECT

**"WE'RE EXCITED!"**

Do you remember what it felt like when you and your mate found out you were expecting? Or when you received the news you had been matched with a child through adoption? Relive this special time in your life. If your spouse is with you, do this activity together.

**How did you find out?**

**What were you feeling?**

**Who did you tell?**

**How did you prepare?**

However the news first reached you that you were to become a parent, nothing would ever be the same. Nothing *could* ever be the same. God was entrusting the care of a new life into your hands.

**Share some of the details of that day with your group. What similarities do you see in everyone's story?**

Along with increasing nervousness, you no doubt experienced immense joy at the impending arrival of your first child. When that child finally arrived, you were forever changed. He stole your heart. She introduced daily wonder and adventure. You would do anything for your children.

**FAST-FORWARD TO TODAY**

Let's be honest: Parenting is a demanding endeavor. You never clock out. Whenever you feel like you have made it through one set of challenges, something else looms around the corner, waiting to launch you on a new adventure or stop you in your tracks.

**What word or phrase best describes last week for you as a parent?**

If "I'm exhausted!" popped out of your mouth, you are not alone. While you still love your children, the hectic pace of life sometimes robs you of the time to be intentional in your parenting. Instead of joy filling your heart, anxiousness may be taking over. Where excitement once abounded in your relationship with your children, stress and friction sometimes are more apparent.

**How do you feel about your parenting at this time?**

**How do you talk about your children around others?**

Exhaustion is not every parent's modus operandi, of course. You may be in a sweet spot with your children, but still know how easy it is to slip back into a frenetic pace. *The Love Dare for Parents* journey is a look at parenting as Scripture describes it—at loving our children the way God does. It's about walking in a relationship with the One who created us and entrusted our kids to us. This relational walk may result in conviction and in needed change in perspective and action. So what are we waiting for?

# RETHINK

## RUNNING RAGGED

In today's society, parents can easily become distracted and obsessed with the relentless pursuit of worthless things, much like the ancient builders of the tower of Babel: "Come, let us build our-selves a city and a tower with its top in the sky. Let us make a name for ourselves" (Gen. 11:4). Their efforts proved vain. God humbled their taxing, misguided attempt. Seeking after bigger and better "towers" can still happen when we are least aware.

With good intentions, many parents believe that the best way to show their children love is through provision. Others feel that the most loving action is to equip their children for worldly applause and financial success. While these may be good pursuits, they are not necessarily the best.

Psalm 127, a worship song, is attributed to Solomon. Let's see what this wise king had to say about God's rightful place in the home.

> **Read Psalm 127:1-2.**
> *Unless the LORD builds a house, its builders labor over it in vain;*
> *unless the LORD watches over a city, the watchman stays alert*
> *in vain. In vain you get up early and stay up late, working hard*
> *to have enough food—yes, He gives sleep to the one He loves.*

The word *vain* means "empty" or "worthless."

**Do some of your parental pursuits seem empty or worthless? What might need to change?**

Many parents recognize themselves in verse 2—getting up early, staying up late, and frantic in between. At the same time, they should be encouraged and refreshed that God "gives sleep," or true rest (see Prov. 3:24). Solomon provides this dual reminder of the need for God to be central in the home and the caution to avoid chasing the wrong prizes and setting the wrong priorities.

---

Psalm 127:2 is a call for dependence on God as well as a commitment to family. It is not an excuse for laziness. Scripture is clear concerning the value of hard work (Prov. 6:6-11; 10:26; 13:4; 19:24; 24:30; 26:14-16).

---

## REAL REWARDS

"A house is built by wisdom, and it is established by under-standing; by knowledge the rooms are filled with every precious and beautiful treasure" (Prov. 24:3-4). God is the architect of the home and parents are laborers with Him. A foundation estab-lished on His Word is strong and lasting, in contrast to a flashy tower meant to glorify ourselves or satisfy worldly desires.

In Psalm 127:1 the term *watchman* describes a sentinel guarding the walls of an ancient city. Instead of being under the care of an impersonal guard, we have the opportunity to know God person-ally and partner with Him. We can wear ourselves out striving and worrying about our children, but if God is not involved in the building and protection of them, our efforts are in vain.

As we learn more of Him through His Word and intentionally make Him the head of our home, He gives rest and direction. Instead of anxious toil without God's leading, true joy can be found in our homes and earthly pursuits by walking in a holy relation-ship with Him. (See Ps. 128:1-4; 1 Cor. 3:9-11.)

> **Read Psalm 127:3.**
>
> *Sons are indeed a heritage from the* LORD, *children, a reward.*

Unlike our tendency to build things in our own strength (Gen. 11:1-8), God's desires to bless and use us greatly are often fulfilled through His gift of children. Consider this verse from Genesis 11:27—"These are the family records of Terah. Terah fathered Abram..." from whom many nations and God's covenant people would come.

**In these examples, underline words describing God's blessing and circle words reflecting the parent's view.**

*Sarah:* "By faith even Sarah herself, when she was unable to have children, received power to conceive offspring, even though she was past the age, since she considered that the One who had promised was faithful" (Heb. 11:11).

*Rachel:* "Then God remembered Rachel. He listened to her and opened her womb. She conceived and bore a son, and said, 'God has taken away my shame.' She named him Joseph: 'May the LORD add another son to me'" (Gen. 30:22-24).

*Manoah (Samson's father):* "Then Manoah asked, 'When Your words come true, what will the boy's responsibilities and mission be?'" (Judg. 13:12).

*Hannah:* "I prayed for this boy, and since the LORD gave me what I asked Him for, I now give the boy to the LORD. For as long as he lives, he is given to the LORD" (1 Sam. 1:27-28).

*Zechariah:* "But the angel said to him: 'Do not be afraid, Zechariah, because your prayer has been heard. Your wife Elizabeth will bear you a son, and you will name him John. There will be joy and delight for you, and many will rejoice at his birth'" (Luke 1:13-14).

Did you notice how those who had the hardest time having a child were often more grateful to God for His great gift?

**Describe parental behaviors and attitudes that portray children as either a burden or as a blessing.**

BURDEN                                    BLESSING

Follow up by asking yourself some questions—and taking action:

- Have I been <u>praying</u>, <u>explaining</u>, and <u>training</u> my children to avoid misbehaviors? What is working well? What still needs attention?

- What are my <u>words</u>, <u>tone of voice</u>, and <u>facial expressions</u> communicating—that my kids are a serious burden or a significant blessing?

- How does God <u>view it</u> when I act as if my children are a burden?

## A FAMILY'S BLESSING AND FUTURE

Children are a huge responsibility, but are not intended to be viewed as a burden. They are priceless, desirable, and unique treasures. God made them in His image, created them with a purpose, loves them without limitation, and places them in our care. They are both our inheritance and legacy.

**Read Psalm 127:4-5.**
> *Like arrows in the hand of a warrior are the sons born*
> *in one's youth. Happy is the man who has filled his*
> *quiver with them. Such men will never be put to shame*
> *when they speak with their enemies at the city gate.*

No arrow is initially ready for battle. Each must be shaped and sharpened to be effective.

**How does God use parents to shape and sharpen their children? How do our children shape and sharpen us?**

We lovingly sharpen them by teaching them, protecting them, guiding them, and releasing them. Not only do we sharpen them, they also sharpen us.

They teach us how to stop being selfish and instead love and give sacrificially. They expose our rough edges, showing us what to work on. God uses our children to help conform us to the image of Christ as we learn patience, kindness, love, joy, and faith (see Rom. 12:2; Eph. 2:10). They stretch us, deepen our prayer life, quicken our consciences with their innocence, and teach us about the Word as we explain it to them.

On the archer's battlefield, arrows hit targets far beyond his physical reach. In a similar way, our children can extend the influence and impact of our lives and do more for God's kingdom than we can accomplish in our lifetime. God uses our children to help us fulfill His eternal purposes for our lives in this world.

Our children are like prized, life-preserving arrows in the hands of a warrior, uniquely formed to be launched to make a powerful impact on the world. We have been invited to partner with God to shape and mold our children into mighty instruments for the kingdom of God. What a privilege! What a gift!

# RENEW

*We benefit our children by applying—not just discussing—biblical truths.*
*This section is an opportunity to put biblical truths into practice each week.*
*You can do these actions as a group or as homework if time does not permit.*

**GET SPECIFIC**

1. **REFLECT** by making this statement personal: "Children are a blessing and a gift from God." Write this sentence and replace "children" with the name of each child ("John is a blessing and a gift from God"). Record three ways that child is a blessing to you.

2. **READ** Psalm 112, a foundational passage for this Bible study. Either in class or in your quiet time, think deeply about what verses 1-2 say about how your children are blessed by your spiritual walk with God.

> *Hallelujah! Happy is the man who fears the* LORD,
> *taking great delight in His commands.*
> *His descendants will be powerful in the land; the*
> *generation of the upright will be blessed.*

3. **PRAY** for each child by name every day this week. Thank God for the specific ways he or she is a blessing to you. One goal of this study is to learn how to pray more intentionally for our children, and pages 88-89, "How to Pray for Your Children," are filled with great ideas to get started. You may want to establish groups of 3-4 to pray together for each other's families and children by name, so that by the end of the study, the entire group has prayed for every family.

4. **SURVEY** a few parents whose children are no longer living at home and ask these empty nesters two questions: What is one thing you wish you had done (or done more of) while the kids were still at home? What is the best advice you would give parents for enjoying and training their children? Be ready to share their answers next week.

5. **DARE** to "communicate to your children that they are a treasure to you. In your own words, say, 'You are a priceless gift to me, and I am grateful you are in my life.' Then thank God for them and for the chance He has given you to daily love and value them."—*The Love Dare for Parents*, day 4

6. **OPTION**: Your group members may want to consider using *The Love Dare for Parents* as you go through this study. This exciting 40-day journey highlights powerful biblical principles of parenting while giving moms and dads a daily dare or challenge to help them better express God's love to their children.

You don't have to read *The Love Dare for Parents* to do this Bible study, but reading and doing the dares will give you more ways to love and bless your children. Doing so will also help you come to your small group ready to share rich insights.

Supporting this week's Bible study are days 1-7 of *The Love Dare for Parents*: *Love blooms; Love is patient, Love is kind, Love values, Love is wonderful, Love is not selfish,* and *Love is not irritable.* (Also see pp. 86-87.)

## Session 2

# Specific Masterpiece

To really know and love
your children means getting
to know and love the One
who created them.

# REFLECT

To say your child is unique may seem trite, but your child really *is* unbelievably special. God does not make any carbon copies.

> Every child is a one of a kind mini-masterpiece. No known duplicates exist. They each have distinctive fingerprints, heart rhythms, eye patterns, and blood constitution. Even identical twins can be physically alike and yet light years apart in how they are mentally wired and gifted. Our children do not just *grow up* different; they *show up* different. —*The Love Dare for Parents*, day 5

God's design of each child includes the uniqueness of gender, birth order, intelligence, love language, talents, abilities, personality, dreams, and passions. As your child grows, you will begin to see distinctive ways he or she shows selfishness and sin.

**Share a distinctive fact or characteristic about each child. (Avoid embarrassing your kids.)**

**Read Ephesians 2:10. What reason does this verse give as to why God has made us unique?**
> *For we are His creation, created in Christ Jesus for good works, which God prepared ahead of time so that we should walk in them.*

Because each child is different, wise parents will adapt their parenting to best meet the needs of each child. Learning how God has distinctively wired each child can help you tailor the way you discipline, show affection, and teach life lessons.

# RETHINK

The love parents have for their children is one of the strongest of all human emotions. The Greek word *storge* (STOR-gay) describes the family love and natural affection we feel for blood relatives, especially our children.

One of the keys to successful parenting is to let sincere love become our primary motivation for what we do regarding our children. But too often we depend on our feelings and the wrong kind of love. Our parental love is limited by our humanity and polluted by our sinfulness.

A stronger love exists—one that is unstoppable because "it bears all things, believes all things, hopes all things, endures all things" (1 Cor. 13:7). The Greek word *agape* (uh-GAHP-ay) refers to the love God commands us to demonstrate most often. A*gape* is not based on feelings, circumstances, or the behavior of the one being loved.

The key to loving our children with *agape* love is not to try harder, but to tap into its pure and perfect source, which is God Himself (1 John 4:7). By connecting to Him and His never-ending supply, the love we have for our children can actually be God's love for them. First John 3:1 states, "Look at how great a love [*agape*] the Father has given us that we should be called God's children."

Learning to love our children is based in receiving God's love, loving Him back, and reflecting His nature. To model love and godliness and launch our children well requires that we stay personally connected to Him and uniquely focused on them, and allow Him to help us better understand and uniquely parent each individual.

## AFFIRMING UNIQUENESS (Ps. 139:1-6,13-16)

As parents learn to walk more closely with God, they will discover how involved He currently is in their children's lives.

> **Turn to Psalm 139. Someone read verses 1-6 aloud while you listen for descriptions of God's omnipresence. What do these verses say about how intimately God knows you and each of your children?**

This psalm paints a beautiful picture of God's constant presence in our lives. He created us, knows us intimately, and cares for us.

> **As a masterpiece yourself, how are you personally reassured by these verses? As a parent of a masterpiece, how does this passage encourage you?**

God is both majestic in nature, beyond our reach and understanding, and intimately involved in our lives: "You have encircled me; You have placed Your hand on me" (v. 5).

**Read Psalm 139:13-16.**

> *For it was You who created my inward parts;*
> *You knit me together in my mother's womb.*
> *I will praise You because I have been remarkably and*
> *wonderfully made. Your works are wonderful, and I know this*
> *very well. My bones were not hidden from You when I was*
> *made in secret, when I was formed in the depths of the earth.*
> *Your eyes saw me when I was formless; all my days were written*
> *in Your book and planned before a single one of them began.*

**Practically, how do you get closer to the One who knows your child best?**

Your child was handmade by God, knit together before you ever laid eyes on him (v. 13). The individual intricacies that distinguish one child from another were God's idea and plan. His eyes saw your child before there was anything to actually see (v. 16)!

If you want to really understand and love your children, then spend time with the One who created them and knows each of them, and you, best.

**For what are you most thankful regarding how God has "remarkably and wonderfully made" your children (v. 14)? What might you specifically point out to each child?**

God has already recorded in His book every day of your child's life before it happens (v. 16). He chooses people for callings, vocations, and missions before they are born (Jer. 1:5).

> **As you consider God's unique design of each of your children, what might He be calling them to do for Him one day? Why should we teach our children to use their giftedness to serve the needs of others? (Also see 1 Pet. 4:10-11.)**

Whoever has your children's hearts has their ears and significantly influences the direction of their lives. If you lose their hearts, your children are likely to turn away from you in the long run. While God is calling them, other forces are at work as well.

> **What are those forces for each of your children? What are you doing to protect them and keep their hearts?**

Winning and keeping your children's hearts does not mean cowering, obeying their every whim or fancy, or giving them whatever they want. It means being connected to God and focused on them, valuing and protecting them as treasures. It means providing the loving attention, affection, and affirmation your children need while carefully guarding against emotional distance, hurts, or unresolved issues coming between you.

**Have you done anything that has caused you to lose your child's heart? If so, consider apologizing and asking for forgiveness in order to rebuild a heart-to-heart relationship with your child.**

## DISCIPLING PERSONALLY (Ps. 139:23-24)

Because children are unique, parenting well requires different approaches. Discipline that works on one child may not phase another, while efforts to make one child feel loved may not work as well on another.

Ultimately, your job as a parent is to make strong disciples of your children. Discipleship is that process of developing spiritual infants into spiritually mature adults, growing them up in the faith—helping them become like Jesus Christ.

No one made disciples better than Jesus Himself. His goal was the same but His approach differed with the person. When relating to Peter, Jesus often used a bold rebuke to get his attention (Matt. 16:23). With James and John, He questioned their desires in order to get to the heart of their thinking (Matt. 20:22). For Thomas, Jesus offered him the proof he so earnestly desired (John 20:27).

Jesus' intentionality worked. Peter, once known for cowardice (John 18:16-18), would be remembered for boldness in preaching the gospel (Acts 4:19-20). John, once called "Son of Thunder" for wanting to call down fire on the unrepentant (Luke 9:54), would become known as the disciple who taught Christians to "love one another" (1 John 3:11).

Jesus loved the disciples as they were while cultivating them distinctively according to God's purpose. Acknowledging how God has shaped our children, we are to both affirm who they are and guide them toward who they could become in Christ.

If your goal for parenting is for your children to make you look good, then you're likely missing out on some abundant life with your family. If your goal is to help them become more like Jesus, then you are joining God in what He desires and is already doing (see Rom. 8:28-29).

**Read and pray Psalm 139:23-24.**

*Search me, God, and know my heart;*
*test me and know my concerns.*
*See if there is any offensive way in me;*
*lead me in the everlasting way.*

**What weakness, "offensive way," or vulnerability do you see in your children? How are you helping them redirect their steps and guard their hearts?**

**How is God convicting and testing *you*? What solution does the psalmist lift up in verse 24?**

We mirror for our family a growing relationship with God when we yield to His convicting of sin, repent, and seek a pure heart and His everlasting way above all.

## TEACHING WHAT MATTERS MOST

At the deepest levels of our love for our children is a desire to understand and teach them what matters most in life. And when everything is stripped away, one truth remains: God created us and our children with an eternal purpose in mind—to become His children, to know and express His *agape* love, to honor Him with our lives, and to spend eternity with Him (John 3:16).

You may not have come to this study knowing God on a personal level. You may not have experienced the forgiveness that comes from accepting Christ's sacrifice for you on the cross. If so, that can change at this moment. You don't need to understand everything about God to reach out in trust to Him. (See pp. 82-83.)

Likewise, you don't have to know everything to share God's love with your kids. The Lord has loved them from "before the foundation of the world" (Eph. 1:4) and, in His love, He graciously invites us to participate with Him at every step along their way.

No matter whether your children are strong-willed or compliant, it is extremely difficult to shape the character of children who don't have the Spirit of God in them. How are they introduced to that Spirit? By turning from their own sin and placing their faith in God's Son. They learn much about God's nature as you show love to them. They discover how special Jesus is when you tell them and show them how special He is to you every day.

---

Our children need to humbly realize that they
are sinners, but still see themselves as beloved by
God, made in His image, and blessed by you, their
parents. —*The Love Dare for Parents*, day 12

---

Some parents teach the fruit of the Spirit (Gal. 5:22-23) or characteristics of love (1 Cor. 13:4-7) to improve behavior. While children may show signs of patience or kindness or self-control, if they are not born again, they are incapable of maintaining godly living since His Spirit does not live in them.

Agreed, your child is a masterpiece designed by God; but you must come to grips with the fact that, without a personal relationship with Jesus, your child is lost (Heb. 11:6) and dead in sin (Eph. 2:1). Your ultimate goal is not behavior modification but heart transformation and salvation.

As a parent, you allow God's Holy Spirit to work in you as you lay spiritual foundations for your children. As you are faithful, authentic, and prayerful in your relationship with God, you can share the good news of Jesus with your children. God desires to use the example of your life as He opens their eyes to understand and respond to Him personally.

As He stirs your children's hearts, God will open doors of conversation and give you the privilege of showing them how to turn to Him and freely place their lives in His hands. At that moment, He will place His Spirit into them. This experience is one of the greatest joys in life and the highest priority of parenting.

> *Permit the children to come to Me; do not hinder them; for the kingdom of God belongs to such as these (Mark 10:14, NASB).*

# RENEW

*Celebrate your masterpieces as you apply biblical truth.*

**GET SPECIFIC**

1. **REFLECT** on how you can share love with your children. What do they need to hear from you to win their hearts? How can you show them your love?

2. **READ** Psalm 112:3-4 and pray about your home becoming a place where grace, compassion, and righteousness abound. Ask that God would one day make your children lights in this world for His glory.

> *Wealth and riches are in his house, and*
> *his righteousness endures forever.*
> *Light shines in the darkness for the upright.*
> *He is gracious, compassionate, and righteous.*

**READ** Galatians 5:22-25. What is the true source of love and other character traits we seek as parents? Which fruit of the Spirit do you most need in your parenting now? What do verses 24-25 say you must do to live in God's Spirit? How does this impact your parenting?

> *Now those who belong to Christ Jesus have crucified*
> *the flesh with its passions and desires.*
> *Since we live by the Spirit, we must also follow the Spirit.*

3. **PRAY** about each child's salvation and spiritual growth. Ask God to open the hearts of your children to learn to love Him. Pray that He would give you clarity for seeing how the Holy Spirit is at work among your children. Keep godly conversation and a listening ear an active part of your parenting.

4. **SURVEY** your children to find out what words and demonstrations of love are the most meaningful. Begin communicating in more of those ways more often. Look for differences your communication makes in your relationship.

5. **DARE** to take a significant step as you "reach out to your children one by one, and tell them you want to be closer to them than you are right now. Ask them questions: 'Have I hurt you or wronged you in any way? Are you angry with me? How can I make it right? Help me understand what's going on inside you' ... Begin taking steps toward winning and keeping their hearts."
—*The Love Dare for Parents*, day 8

6. **OPTION**: Read days 8-15 in *The Love Dare for Parents* to better understand this week's lesson: *Love wins, Love cherishes, Love is not rude, Love teaches, Love encourages, Love disciplines, Love is compassionate*, and *Love is from God*. (Also see pp. 86-87.)

## SESSION 3

# Secure Boundaries

Setting secure boundaries
gives children a better
chance at holy living.

# REFLECT

**PARENTAL PRECAUTIONS**

"You'll understand when you have children of your own." Children of all generations have accused their parents of being unfair and out of touch because of the rules they set. Many parents opt out of an argument by explaining that kids will understand better when they have children of their own. We hope.

**What rules did your parents have that you couldn't stand (or understand) when you were a child?**

**How do you feel now that you're a parent?**

Over time, our perspective changes. We begin to sound like our mothers or do things like our fathers. Because love always protects (see 1 Cor. 13:7), we tolerate weekly sighs and rolling eyes, knowing that our children will likely say thank you one day and set similar standards for *their* children.

**What are some types of loving boundaries needed at these stages for your children?**

**Newborn**

**Toddler**

**Elementary-school-age**

**Teenager**

Everyone has three distinct aspects to his or her total being. Look
for them in this verse:

> *Now may the God of peace Himself sanctify you completely. And*
> *may your spirit, soul, and body be kept sound and blameless*
> *for the coming of our Lord Jesus Christ (1 Thess. 5:23).*

Our job is to protect our children spiritually, emotionally, and
physically until they are able to protect themselves. We do so by
providing secure boundaries in which we safeguard them from
physical harm, mental and emotional danger, and any spiritual
influence that is contrary to the Word of God. Let's make the
boundaries clear and loving.

# RETHINK

In 1 Samuel 3, we read of God's calling of Samuel, whom God would use to bless the nation of Israel. Hannah, Samuel's mother, had prayed earnestly for a child. When Samuel was born, Hannah dedicated him to the Lord and to serve under Eli, the priest who had blessed her in her fervent prayer to conceive a child (1 Sam. 1:26-28; 1 Sam. 1:17).

Eli was leading Israel's worship at this time, but his sons would not continue his legacy. At the time God was calling Samuel to minister, He was rejecting the actions of Eli and his sons.

**INTERVENTION OMISSION (1 Sam. 3:10-18)**
**Someone read 1 Samuel 3:10-18 aloud. What sins were Eli's sons committing, according to verse 13? Why was this so serious?**


**Though Eli was not committing these sins, why was God upset with him (v. 13)?**


In 1 Samuel 2 Eli's sons were classified as "wicked men; they had no regard for the LORD" (2:12). They were defiling the worship of God, committing sexual immorality, and practicing evil (see 1 Sam. 2:12-17,22-23). God held Eli responsible for neglecting to address his sons' sinful lifestyle even in adulthood. Instead of rebuking them, Eli had placed his blind love for them ahead of God's call to train his sons before the Lord. Like Eli, when we refuse to discipline, our long-term love is ultimately in question.

Other families in the Bible experienced conflict when their children decided to reject God. Jacob suffered hardship (Gen. 34:30) and heartache (Gen. 37:33-36) because he was ignorant about his sons' deceptive dealings. Job was known to sacrifice extra offerings just in case his children had sinned or cursed God (Job 1:5). Church leadership in the New Testament was restricted to those who were able to manage "his own household competently, having his children under control with all dignity" (1 Tim. 3:4; compare to 3:12; Titus 1:6).

Parents should prayerfully set well-defined and clear boundaries. We should communicate to our children that God has entrusted them to us and that we will be held accountable by God for our watch over their souls (see Heb. 13:17). When boundaries are crossed, loving parents must step in with appropriate discipline.

Creating boundaries gives children stability and helps them grasp the gravity of sin. If our children are to become godly adults, we need to be involved in their daily lives when they are young—listening and engaging in conversations, staying in touch with their friendships and activities, and watching for signs of sin creeping in or external dangers or internal rebellion.

To mold our children in such a way that they desire holiness, we must teach them to fear God, honor their parents, and respect the boundaries we set for them.

THE
Love Dare
FOR PARENTS BIBLE STUDY

### FEAR GOD (Deut. 6:1-3)

*This is the command—the statues and ordinances—the* LORD *your God has instructed me to teach you, so that you may follow them in the land you are about to enter and possess.*

*Do this so that you may fear the* LORD *your God all the days of your life by keeping all His statutes and commands I am giving you, your son, and your grandson, and so that you may have a long life.*

*Listen, Israel, and be careful to follow them, so that you may prosper and multiply greatly, because Yahweh, the God of your fathers, has promised you a land flowing with milk and honey.*

Continuing to teach to the very end, Moses instructed the children of Israel as to how they should live once they entered the promised land. The Israelites were to be characterized by a fear of the Lord if they were to obtain genuine prosperity and God's blessing.

While many today shy away from the concept of fearing God, it is a repeated biblical instruction. In Jesus' ministry of grace He still emphasized, "Don't fear those who kill the body but are not able to kill the soul; rather, fear Him who is able to destroy both soul and body in hell" (Matt. 10:28).

---

A healthy fear of the Lord is the foundational key that enables our children to think more wisely, speak more honorably, and live in a way that's more pleasing to God. —*The Love Dare for Parents*, day 16

---

**According to these verses, what does it mean for one to have a healthy fear of God?**
**Psalm 34:11-14**

**Proverbs 8:13**

**Proverbs 14:27**

The fear of the Lord is not anxious terror, but reverential respect. It acknowledges God as completely holy, just, and omniscient. A healthy fear involves seeking God, not fleeing from Him. It affirms His love and His correction when we turn from Him. It means turning away from evil and seeking, even rejoicing in, the truth.

Fearing the Lord means obeying His commands and walking in His ways. The fear of the Lord awakens wisdom and discernment within us and our children as we realize that we are living in a universe completely under His control.

## HONOR PARENTS (Eph. 6:1-4)

> *Children, obey your parents in the Lord, because this is right. Honor your father and mother, which is the first commandment with a promise, so that it may go well with you and that you may have a long life in the land. Fathers, don't stir up anger in your children, but bring them up in the training and instruction of the Lord.*

**How does teaching your children to fear the Lord and honor their parents and other authority figures set them up for lifelong success (also see Heb. 13:17)?**

Training our children to respect and obey us now prepares them to respect and obey God as teenagers and adults. As the Bible explains, when parents and their children learn to fear the Lord, they begin to hate evil, pride, and perversion (see Prov. 8:13) and avoid the "snares of death" (Prov. 14:27). This fear helps a little girl stop lying and a teenage boy quit acting immorally, as they realize a holy God sees them and will judge them one day.

In the Ephesians 6 verses, the apostle Paul singled out fathers for some advice. Fathers were meant to point their children to God without exasperating them.

**How are you and your spouse handling the balance of training without overly frustrating your children?**

---

Gradually allow your children to test new waters with wisdom. Protectiveness is not merely restriction. It's not just avoiding the negative and letting nothing come along to fill its place. —*The Love Dare for Parents*, day 19

---

**How are you helping your children understand that your protection is not merely restriction, but for their greater good?**

While godly protection does restrict, it also replaces. It overcomes the tide of evil in culture with a tidal wave of good (Rom. 12:21). It surrounds kids with good books, great music, and godly friends. It helps them learn "*the difference* between the holy and the profane ... to discern between the unclean and the clean" (Ezek. 44:23, NASB). It presses pause on the remote to talk openly about what was right or wrong about that last movie scene. By helping kids learn to discern and by strengthening their resistance skills, you equip them with the protection they'll need when they leave your watch.

**BUILD BOUNDARIES (Prov. 1:8; 6:32; 10:4; 13:20)**
For now, your children are still in your home and you have the responsibility to help them set limits. The Book of Proverbs, full of great counsel, is primarily a collection of sayings from Solomon when he was offering his son wise advice for living.

> **Define the boundary set by each verse.**
> *The one who walks with the wise will become wise,*
> *but a companion of fools will suffer harm* (Prov. 13:20).
> **Boundary**: _____
>
> *The one who commits adultery lacks sense;*
> *whoever does so destroys himself* (Prov. 6:32).
> **Boundary**: _____
>
> *Idle hands make one poor, but diligent*
> *hands bring riches* (Prov. 10:4).
> **Boundary**: _____

Did you notice how Solomon tackled adult issues ahead of time, to prepare his son for the temptations he would certainly encounter?

Sometimes protective boundaries need to be set in advance to prepare children; sometimes boundaries are set after an area of weakness or stumbling is exposed. The discussion and decisions that take place now regarding friendship, morality, and personal responsibility will greatly impact your children in the future.

**How are you realizing the importance of setting boundaries at different ages and stages?**

**What biblical and practical boundaries has your family already set to guard your children? Share your answers with the group.**

**What areas of weakness or stumbling have revealed some new protective boundaries you might need to establish for your children?**

**Read Hebrews 3:13. How can a parent's daily encouragement help his or her children avoid the deceptions of sin?**

Boundaries are not designed to take away freedom, but to guard and protect liberty in the long run, so that our children will be safe and free to do the will of God for their lives.

# RENEW

*It's time to apply what we have learned.*

**GET SPECIFIC**

1. **REFLECT** on areas of concern you have for each child physically, emotionally, or spiritually. Be specific.

2. **PRAY** for each of your children today and this week, focusing on these specific concerns. Pray that your children would avoid sin's traps. Also ask God for His wisdom in setting boundaries.

3. **READ** verses 5-6 of Psalm 112. What legacy is promised for the one who is righteous? How do right attitudes reflect themselves in right actions?

> *Good will come to a man who lends generously and*
> *conducts his business fairly. He will never be shaken.*
> *The righteous man will be remembered forever.*

4. **SURVEY** parents you respect concerning the types of boundaries they have set for their children. Find out what has worked and what these parents would suggest. Prayerfully consider whether some might be appropriate for your home.

5. **DARE** to talk with your spouse "about setting the appropriate boundaries for your children regarding access to the Internet, television, movies, and phone use. Prayerfully draw up guidelines for what kind of activities are allowable with their friends. Before you present your decisions to them, pray for discernment and for the Lord to work in both your heart and your children's."
—*The Love Dare for Parents*, day 19

6. **OPTION**: Days 16-21 in *The Love Dare for Parents* complement this week's lesson: *Love respects God, Love seeks God's blessing, Love models the way, Love protects, Love takes time,* and *Love is fair.* (Also see pp. 86-87.)

SESSION 4

*Serious Responsibility*

Your children will learn more
by how you live
than by what you say.

# REFLECT

## ENJOYING FAMILY RESEMBLANCES

Family portraits are such treasures, documenting the family's experiences from year to year. As you flip through albums or watch slideshows, you likely are amazed at how everyone has changed.

**Describe family resemblances—physical and lifestyle similarities—that have clearly been passed down from parents to children.**

**In what ways are your children like you in what they say or do?**

Some of those similarities are due to nature and some are attributed to nurture. Some are amusing while others reflect issues you wish your children had not picked up from you.

## "SIMON SAYS"

Do you remember the children's game "Simon Says"? This mimicking game tricks players as the momentum builds. If the leader doesn't start instructions with "Simon Says," then followers are not to do the action. What makes this game both fun and frustrating is that we are more prone to do what we see than what we hear—even if the instructions are otherwise.

---

What happens with your children at home will follow
them everywhere. —*The Love Dare for Parents*, day 22

---

That's why a parent's relationship with the Lord is so vital to a
child's spiritual health. No one influences your children more than
you do. And no matter what you tell your children, your example is
what they will follow, even when it contradicts what you say. Your
children will learn more by how you live than by what you say.

# RETHINK

While many religious leaders have said, "Follow my teaching,"
Jesus Christ said, "Follow Me!" He privately practiced and daily
modeled what He publicly taught. In the days before His arrest and
crucifixion, He told His disciples, "For I have given you an example
that you also should do just as I have done for you" (John 13:15).

As parents, we must consistently model the behavior we request
and hope to see in our children. The apostle Paul told his spiritual
children, "Do what you have learned and received and heard and
seen in me" (Phil. 4:9).

**If your children daily practiced what they have seen
in you, would it be a good thing or a bad thing?**

During Jesus' last days on earth, someone asked Him who would
be greatest in the kingdom of heaven. His answer provides insight
into our example for our children.

## HOW SERIOUSLY DO YOU TAKE YOUR PARENTING? (Matt. 18:1-9)

**Read Matthew 18:1-5.**

*At that time, the disciples came to Jesus and said,*
*"Who is greatest in the kingdom of heaven?"*
*Then He called a child to Him and had him stand among them.*
*"I assure you," He said, "unless you are converted and become*
*like children, you will never enter the kingdom of heaven.*
*Therefore, whoever humbles himself like this child—*
*this one is the greatest in the kingdom of heaven.*
*And whoever welcomes one child like this*
*in My name welcomes Me."*

**What does this passage reveal about Jesus' heart for children? About the childlike faith connected to true conversion? About attitudes and personal example?**

Jesus' nature, as well as His words, attracted people, including children. When the disciples attempted to run off people who were bringing their children to Jesus, He rebuked them (Mark 10:13-16). Jesus loved children. He spoke to them, embraced them, affirmed them, and blessed them.

**Read Matthew 18:6-9 to see how seriously Jesus takes our examples.**

*But whoever causes the downfall of one of these little
ones who believe in Me—it would be better for him
if a heavy millstone were hung around his neck
and he were drowned in the depths of the sea!
Woe to the world because of offenses. For offenses must
come, but woe to that man by whom the offense comes.
If your hand or your foot causes your downfall, cut
it off and throw it away. It is better for you to enter
life maimed or lame, than to have two hands or
two feet and be thrown into the eternal fire.
And if your eye causes your downfall, gouge it out and
throw it away. It is better for you to enter life with one eye,
rather than to have two eyes and be thrown into hellfire.*

**What did Jesus say would be preferable to a child's
experiencing downfall? What does this mean in a
practical sense?**

Jesus despises it when someone causes a child
to stumble or turn away from God.

**Did you ever observe inconsistent or sinful behavior
in your parents while growing up? How did that
influence your desire to either walk with or turn away
from God?**

**What are the challenges for the child who experiences a parent's moral failure?**

The parent who walks away from the Lord gives an example that, if repeated by his or her children, can lead to generations of pain in this life and misery in the next. Our children will encounter heartache and disappointments, but an introduction to sin and its consequences should not come from their parents!

**Read Exodus 20:4-6 for how generations of children were affected by their parents' obeying or disobeying God.**

*Do not make an idol for yourself . . . You must not bow down to them or worship them; for I, the LORD your God, am a jealous God, punishing the children for the fathers' sin, to the third and fourth generations of those who hate Me, but showing faithful love to a thousand generations of those who love Me and keep My commands.*

We've all seen children who have greatly suffered because of their parents' ungodly decisions. As many as four generations can feel the effects of a legacy of sin, according to this passage. But, more powerfully, the legacy of faithful love can last more than a thousand generations!

Every person has sinned against God and made mistakes. But there is great hope for the future because of God's mercy to forgive and His grace to heal if we fully repent and choose to walk with Him. Your walk with God can literally turn your family around, both now and in the future.

## WHAT EXAMPLE ARE YOU MODELING?

Both parents can and should model healthy relationships. Your words and attitudes should help your children respect the other parent more, not less. Make "honor your father and your mother" (Ex. 20:12) easy for your children to do.

Your kids know when Mom and Dad aren't getting along. They are watching to see how you work things out and to understand what marital mercy looks like. They overhear you talk about coworkers, dysfunctional neighbors, and difficult people.

They learn your extended family's epic saga of who did what to whom and why you intentionally never get around to seeing certain people at holidays anymore.

Your children are learning from you how to either dig in their heels and find a reason to remain bitter or to extend the loving grace that God extends to us, overcoming their greatest obstacles with forgiveness and peacemaking.

> **What do you think would be different if your kids routinely saw you tackle relational train wrecks with relentless love?**

Children stand and grow on the foundation of their parents' relationship. The more you show genuine love and respect for your mate or your ex, the stronger and more loved your children will feel. Being faithful, warm, understanding, and cooperative with

your wife or husband may not always be easy, but it will cash out in your children's hearts as security, peace, strength, and greater self-acceptance.

Our personal examples set the tone. Are we loving and respectful toward each other as husband and wife—forgiving, patient, and kind? Are we showing our kids how to love a woman, how to respect a man, and how to treat the opposite sex by the way we cherish one another?

One of love's high-level jobs is to show our children that while no marriage is perfect, all marriages can be loving. Even if you're a single adult or a divorced parent, you can look for ways to live out and encourage the biblical standards of love, purity, and faithfulness you desire for them.

It is OK to respectfully disagree behind closed doors, but a father and mother need to operate in agreement when they are in front of their children, because you are defining the concepts of marriage, unity, communication, and reconciliation in their growing minds.

They will naturally tend to follow your example—whether it is one of love or bitterness. And they will tend to pass your example on to your grandchildren and great-grandchildren.

ARE YOU MODELING A GROWING
RELATIONSHIP WITH GOD? (Deut. 6:5-7)

**Read the highlighted statement from _The Love Dare
for Parents_. Do you agree or disagree? Explain why.**

---

We must commit to exemplifying a life that lines up
with our words, not only until the temperature in the
house comes back down, but with ongoing, prayerful
dependence on God. We're not just confessing; we're
changing. —_The Love Dare for Parents_, day 25

---

**How do the people in your home benefit if you are
walking closely with God?**

**Read Deuteronomy 6:5-7.**
_Love the LORD your God with all your heart, with all your soul,
and with all your strength. These words that I am giving you
today are to be in your heart. Repeat them to your children. Talk
about them when you sit in your house and when you walk
along the road, when you lie down and when you get up._

**What is significant about the order of the
instructions in this passage?**

**How can you show your vibrant love for the Lord to your children? How could doing so impact their spiritual direction and even future generations?**

Everybody in your home benefits from parents who are fully enjoying their relationship with God. When you surrender control and let God fill you with His love, then the patience, joy, and kindness welling up inside you will pour out onto your family.

When the apostle Paul wrote, "Imitate me, as I also imitate Christ" (1 Cor. 11:1), he gave us a beautiful picture of solid spiritual leadership—and the challenge from all parents to their children.

# RENEW

*Let's renew our minds as we put biblical truth into practice.*

## GET SPECIFIC

1. **REFLECT** on whether you need to confess anything to your children. Have they seen sin in your life for which you need to apologize? Are there areas you need to change? Record your thoughts and commit to act on them.

2. **PRAY** about these areas. Ask God for strength to ask for forgiveness from your children and to make changes where necessary. Pray that your children will see God's Spirit at work in you.

3. **READ** verses 7-8 of Psalm 112. What is the difference between fearing the Lord and fearing circumstances?

> *He will not fear bad news; his heart is*
> *confident, trusting in the* LORD.
> *His heart is assured; he will not fear.*
> *In the end he will look in triumph on his foes.*

4. **SURVEY** someone you respect as a spiritual mentor and guide. Find out how he or she is accomplishing the goal to grow in personal commitment to Christ.

5. **DARE** to "spend time alone with God, reading Jesus' words from Matthew 11:28-30. Instead of routine requests, ask how you can come to Him daily and find rest for your soul. Open up your heart and ask Him to fill you with His love and joy, learning how to find your heart's delight through a more intimate walk with Him.

"Thank Him for His goodness and provision in your life. Enjoy your time being centered on Him. Then let your kids see the difference this makes in you today." —*The Love Dare for Parents*, day 27

6. **OPTION:** Days 22-28 in *The Love Dare for Parents* provide additional insights for this week's lesson: *Love honors authority, Love intercedes, Love forgives, Love takes responsibility, Love is Jesus Christ, Love is satisfied in God,* and *Love is God's Word.* (Also see pp. 86-87.)

## SESSION 5

### *Shared Path*

The best directions come
from someone who has
already traveled the way.

# REFLECT

### DELETED SCENES

**What is your favorite movie and why?**

A popular feature of many DVDs is the inclusion of deleted scenes. These scenes were scripted, recorded, and edited, but for various reasons, never made it into the final release.

**Do you ever wish your life had some deleted scenes?**

We all have wanted to erase a scene due to bad "acting" or the nature of the situation. We wish we could relive and "do over" certain experiences. We have endured circumstances we wish had never been part of our lives.

Unless you want your children's "movie" to be a remake of your "classic," you must be intentional about helping your children navigate safely and wisely through life.

### DIRECTOR'S CUT

We are called to warn our children about pitfalls and point them toward safe havens. At the same time, they *will* encounter difficult circumstances sooner or later. We cannot keep them from experiencing pain, but we can prepare them to understand and deal with it. We cannot keep our children from sin, but we can show them a better way and equip them to face and withstand temptation.

Love doesn't wait for the fires of life to consume our
families; it installs smoke detectors and sprinkler
heads beforehand. —*The Love Dare for Parents*, day 32

Parents are wise to equip their children with adequate lessons,
networks, and influences that set them up for godly success. Our
children need wise counsel from those of us who have been there
before. Let's prepare the way and lead them well.

# RETHINK

**WORDS TO LIVE BY (1 Kings 2:1-4)**
The psalmist David knew what it was like to endure difficult
seasons of life. Reading the Psalms gives us a front row seat to
the depths of his feelings during the best and the worst of times.
Through successes and failures, he had numerous life lessons to
pass on to future generations.

**As a group, identify some key events in the life of
David. (An example has been done for you.)**

**THE GOOD** (things David did well)
Skilled musician

**THE BAD** (bad things that happened to David)
Chased by a king

**THE UGLY (problems David brought on himself)**
His child's death

---

At no time are their hearts more vulnerable—
or more teachable—than when damaged or
challenged by life's cruel, upsetting, and unwanted
disappointments. —*The Love Dare for Parents*, day 30

---

On his deathbed, David gave his son Solomon some great fatherly
advice to live by in uncertain times.

**Read 1 Kings 2:1-4.**

> As the time approached for David to die, he instructed his
> son Solomon, "As for me, I am going the way of all of the
> earth. Be strong and be courageous like a man, and keep your
> obligation to the LORD your God to walk in His ways and
> to keep His statutes, commands, ordinances, and decrees.
>
> This is written in the law of Moses, so that you will have
> success in everything you do and wherever you turn,
> and so that the LORD will carry out His promise that He
> made to me: 'If your sons are careful to walk faithfully
> before Me with their whole mind and heart, you will
> never fail to have a man on the throne of Israel.'"

When David told Solomon that he was "going the way of all of the earth" (v. 2), what did he mean? Why is this important information to teach our children?

Why should we prepare our children to function well without us?

David also instructed Solomon to obey God's commands (v. 3).

Practically, how can parents help even the youngest child begin to understand and obey God's commands? School-age children? Teenagers? Adult children?

How do our discussions change as we help our children avoid pitfalls and find safe havens throughout their lives?

Being a good parent often means shifting our children toward new expectations, thinking ahead of them when they aren't thinking at all. We're tending to their hearts, not just their hurts, making sure unwelcome changes on the outside can be used by God to

strengthen them on the inside. In so doing, we prepare them for lives of resiliency and grace.

The biblical model of strong leadership is that of a loving shepherd. It's one of constant provision and oversight, managing the day-to-day mechanics of the flock's physical needs. It's a task of tender care and heroic rescue, noticing quickly when the sheep are under duress, frequently scanning the perimeters for predator attacks.

It is a picture of training up and preparing our children to see God as their Shepherd and to follow His voice in the midst of a dark culture (see John 10:4).

> We must never forget that by encouraging our children to walk with God, we are asking them to intentionally travel against the cultural tide. —*The Love Dare for Parents*, day 35

**Define how walking with God differs from walking with the culture.**
**WORLDLY SUCCESS**                    **BIBLICAL SUCCESS**

**In light of your answers, why is it important to mold children to desire biblical success?**

62

David told Solomon that if he lived a life of obedience, he would be successful in everything he did and in every place he went (vv. 3-4). God promised to fulfill His promises and bestow His favor on Solomon and on future generations.

## PATHS TO WALK BY
### Read Proverbs 1:8-10.

> *Listen, my son, to your father's instruction, and don't*
> *reject your mother's teaching, for they will be a garland of*
> *grace on your head and a gold chain around your neck.*
> *My son, if sinners entice you, don't be persuaded.*

**How do you seek to win the trust of your children so they want to hear your instruction?**

## PREPARE THE PATH
Just as you can help your children navigate unknown paths because you've been there and know what to expect, so can other parents help you know what to expect at different stages in parenting.

**Share the next big step you are facing in parenting. Ask for wisdom from others in the group who may have already walked this path.**

**What people or resources can help you prepare for
this part of the journey?**

We want our children ready for life, not merely reacting to it. So
confidently look for opportunities before each new season and
major transition when you can sit down and explain what's coming
up, shedding light on any mysteries in their young minds.

Some of your preparations will highlight significant occasions in
your family: a funeral, a wedding, a rite of passage like learning
to drive. Nearly all provide distinct opportunities to open up the
Scriptures and teach your children more about prayer and learning
to trust God's voice.

### BLESS THE PATH

Throughout Scripture God has set up a pattern of blessing for His
people: verbally affirming His acceptance and support of them,
painting vivid pictures of their hopeful future, and investing
Himself and His resources to make His words a reality.

**Consider ways these parents in the Bible encouraged
and supported their children.**

*Jacob blessed Judah:* "Judah, your brothers will praise
you. Your hand will be on the necks of your enemies;
your father's sons will bow down to you. ... The
scepter will not depart from Judah or the staff from
between his feet until He whose right it is comes
and the obedience of the peoples belongs to Him"
(Gen. 49:8,10).

*David blessed Solomon*: "Now, my son, may the LORD
be with you, and may you succeed in building
the house of the LORD your God, as He said about
you. Above all, may the LORD give you insight and
understanding when He puts you in charge of Israel
so that you may keep the law of the LORD your God"
(1 Chron. 22:11-12).

*God blessed Jesus*: "While he was still speaking, suddenly
a bright cloud covered them, and a voice from the
cloud said: 'This is My beloved Son. I take delight in
Him. Listen to Him!'" (Matt. 17:5).

**What do you notice about these biblical blessings?**

**What kind of blessing do your children need to hear
from you?**

When God blesses us, He is forecasting His favor, guiding us
toward His perfect will and spiritually abundant life. So don't be
afraid to speak your own words of blessing over your children.
Don't fail to cast a vision that spurs them on to consider what
wonderful things God could do in and through them—the lives
they could touch, the difference they could make for the Kingdom.

## PRAY OVER THE PATH

Parents have an opportunity to pray more strategically and lovingly for their children than almost anyone else on earth. As you think about your own children, no matter their ages, how would you pray concerning the following:

**Future spouse**

**Children of their own**

**Church involvement**

**Personal spiritual growth**

**Vocation/calling**

**Influences** (godly friends, mentors, schools, media, and so forth)

# RENEW

*On this shared path, let's apply biblical truths and share wisdom gained.*

**GET SPECIFIC**

1. **REFLECT** on your travel along the parental path. What glaring issues face your home right now? How do you need to prepare yourself to equip your children for upcoming challenges?

2. **PRAY** daily and specifically for your children this week. Use the list of areas you identified in "Pray Over the Path."

3. **SURVEY** issues that children are facing by doing some research. Search Christian websites that educate parents on how to confront the issues your children may encounter with their friends, media, or at school. Be ready to share with your group.

4. **READ** verses 9-10 from Psalm 112. Note the marked contrast between righteousness and wickedness. Ask God to characterize your life and home with righteousness.

> *He distributes freely to the poor;*
> *his righteousness endures forever.*
> *His horn will be exalted in honor.*
> *The wicked man will see it and be angry;*
> *he will gnash his teeth in despair.*
> *The desire of the wicked man will come to nothing.*

5. **DARE** to list important topics you need to discuss with your children: relationships, puberty, integrity, finances, and so forth. Begin planning now for the right time to have these conversations. Then start doing your homework in preparation for those days. Finally, spend time praying for wisdom and guidance. —*The Love Dare for Parents*, day 32

6. **OPTION**: Days 29-35 of *The Love Dare for Parents* provide added insights for this week's lesson: *Love listens, Love shepherds hearts, Love influences, Love prepares, Love blesses, Love and marriage,* and *Love rejoices in truth.* (Also see pp. 86-87.)

### SESSION 6

# Steadfast
# Commitment

While your role as a parent
does change, your love for
your children must endure.

# REFLECT

## STATE OF THE FAMILY

Just as the president of the United States gives an annual State of the Union address to verbalize the country's successes and issues, so the home periodically needs the same attention. First, let's talk about the state of the home in our culture.

**In what areas do you think parents in today's culture need the most improvement?**

**What are some glaring problems concerning children and the home?**

**If you were making a State of the Home address to your family, what key issues would you tackle first and how would you address them?**

Loving our children is a promise, a covenant, a chosen occupation. As times change, the needs of our kids will also change.

Whether you're dealing with training wheels, court-
ship parameters, or money management issues, the
goal is not to check something off your list but to
keep writing key principles across their hearts, year
after year. You're preparing them for life. For success
in every direction. —*The Love Dare for Parents*, day 32

## COMMITTED TO THE END

While you will always be your children's parent, you will not always
parent them the same way. As they grow older, they do not need
you in quite the same ways.

**As your role transitions with your children, to what
are you most looking forward? What do you still
anticipate with a sense of concern?**

As your children grow, develop, and try new things, it is inevitable
that at some time they may disappoint you.

**Is there anything your children could do to make
you love them less? Is your love conditional or
unconditional? Do they know that?**

While your role as a parent will change, your love for your children
must endure. No matter the challenges and opportunities you face,
keep assuring your children of your steadfast commitment to them.

# RETHINK

Our parenting goal from the very beginning is to launch our children well—to prepare them for the day when they will be away from our guidance, responsible for themselves, experiencing success as they try their wings. Much of what we do all along the way is, by design, to teach our kids to function independently and then to leave.

Little by little, especially as our kids begin cycling through the teen years, we need to be intentionally entrusting them with more and more appropriate levels of privilege and responsibility. Larger assignments. Harder jobs. Increasing amounts of freedom. We give it to them carefully—not before they possess the maturity and judgment to carry it, but with a healthy balance of informed release and restraint.

In His own ministry, Jesus was very deliberate about launching His disciples into their future. He gave them clear instructions and encouragement (John 14–17). He promised them His love and the Holy Spirit's ongoing presence. He assured them they were ready, that He had confidence in them. And He prayed with passionate zeal for their protection, success, and influence on the world.

## THE HOPE OF GRACE

Throughout the Gospels, we notice Jesus often being harder on the religious crowd than He was on sinners. (Those who knew Scriptures should have understood grace and been radically changed by it.) In response to criticism that He "welcomes sinners and eats with them" (Luke 15:2), Jesus told three parables to solidify the biblical hope of grace. The parable of the prodigal son is one.

**Ask someone to read Luke 15:11-32 for the entire group. Listen for what this parable teaches us about God and about parenting.**

*He also said: "A man had two sons. The younger of them said to his father, 'Father, give me the share of the estate I have coming to me.' So he distributed the assets to them. Not many days later, the younger son gathered together all he had and traveled to a distant country, where he squandered his estate in foolish living.*

*"After he had spent everything, a severe famine struck that country, and he had nothing. Then he went to work for one of the citizens of that country, who sent him into his fields to feed pigs. He longed to eat his fill from the carob pods the pigs were eating, but no one would give him any. When he came to his senses, he said, 'How many of my father's hired hands have more than enough food, and here I am dying of hunger! I'll get up, go to my father, and say to him, Father, I have sinned against heaven and in your sight. I'm no longer worthy to be called your son. Make me like one of your hired hands.'*

*"So he got up and went to his father. But while the son was still a long way off, his father saw him and was filled with compassion. He ran, threw his arms around his neck, and kissed him. The son said to him, 'Father, I have sinned against heaven and in your sight. I'm no longer worthy to be called your son.'*

"But the father told his slaves, 'Quick! Bring out the best robe and
put it on him; put a ring on his finger and sandals on his feet.
Then bring the fattened calf and slaughter it, and let's celebrate
with a feast, because this son of mine was dead and is alive
again; he was lost and is found!' So they began to celebrate.

"Now his older son was in the field; as he came near the
house, he heard music and dancing. So he summoned one
of the servants and asked what these things meant.
'Your brother is here,' he told him, 'and your father has slaughtered
the fattened calf because he has him back safe and sound.'
Then he became angry and didn't want to go in. So
his father came out and pleaded with him.
But he replied to his father, 'Look, I have been slaving many
years for you, and I have never disobeyed your orders, yet you
never gave me a young goat so I could celebrate with my friends.
But when this son of yours came, who has devoured your assets
with prostitutes, you slaughtered the fattened calf for him.'

"'Son,' he said to him, 'you are always with
me, and everything I have is yours.
But we had to celebrate and rejoice, because this brother of
yours was dead and is alive again; he was lost and is found.'"

**What stands out most to you about this parable?**

**What does this parable say about heaven's definition
of success versus the world's? How can we impart that
distinction to our children?**

While this story ultimately paints a picture of our relationship with God, it does offer some applicable truths for parenting. If we go to anyone for an example of parenting, should we not go *first and foremost* to our Heavenly Father? He is the wisest, most consistent, and most loving parent any child will ever know.

> **In light of the context for this parable, who do the three characters represent?**
> **Father:**
>
>
> **Prodigal Son:**
>
>
> **Older Son:**

This parable is the perfect example of a father who loved both of his children—the one who was faithful and the one who thought he was but needed to deal with resentment and jealousy. This picture of grace helps parents communicate to their children— long before the day they are no longer living in the home—that they will *never* be too far away to come home again.

Your children need to know two things: (1) their decisions bring real consequences and (2) your love for them will never change. Your steadfast commitment to them should be evident from their earliest days of being a part of the family.

As we remind our children of our support and encouragement, we must work to love like our Heavenly Father, accept prodigals as they are, and model grace to all.

### LOVE LIKE OUR HEAVENLY FATHER

**Read Exodus 34:6-7 and Psalm 103:11-13. What do you notice about God as Father?**

*Yahweh is a compassionate and gracious God, slow to anger and rich in faithful love and truth, maintaining faithful love to a thousand generations, forgiving wrongdoing, rebellion, and sin. But He will not leave the guilty unpunished (Ex. 34:6-7).*

*For as high as the heavens are above the earth, so great is His faithful love toward those who fear Him. As far as the east is from the west, so far has He removed our transgressions from us. As a father has compassion on his children, so the LORD has compassion on those who fear Him (Ps. 103:11-13).*

**If you as a parent were to love your children the way God loves His children, what changes would occur?**

### ACCEPT PRODIGALS AS THEY ARE

**Reread Luke 15:14-16. What did you notice about the timing of the prodigal's decision to go home?**

**When should parents lovingly bail out their children, and when should they lovingly allow them to suffer the consequences?**

The balance is tricky. We want to forgive our children when they mess up, but we don't want to allow the sin to go unpunished so they don't understand the nature of consequences. While our Heavenly Father is gracious, He is also wise enough to know that if He doesn't discipline us, we continue to disobey (Heb. 12:7-11).

> The real question is how you will respond if or when your children fail. Love, the Bible says, "bears all things" (1 Cor. 13:7). It endures. Even if the choices made by your kids cause you deep pain and disappointment. —*The Love Dare for Parents*, day 36

Sometimes we have to accept the fact that our children might have to taste sin's harsh consequences and hit rock bottom before they come to their senses and long for a better place (Luke 15:16).

## MODEL GRACE TO ALL
**Read 3 John 1:4.**

*I have no greater joy than this: to hear that my children are walking in the truth.*

**How do you feel when you see or hear that your children are walking in the truth?**

**How do you communicate the deep delight you have in them when your children walk wisely and obediently before God?**

**Remembering the context of this parable (Luke 15:2), who was Jesus rebuking—the prodigal or the older brother? What sin was He confronting?**

**How are you teaching your children to follow God but not to trust in their own attempts at holiness?**

As a parent, you will have moments of great joy and sheer horror over what your children may say or do. Parents are responsible for both the prodigal and the child who appears OK but has spiritual issues that need to be addressed. We must steer carefully and intentionally with the grace that comes only from walking with Jesus.

### PERSONAL EVALUATION

**How has God, your Father, been patient with you?**
**How do you need to change your parenting to better reflect the way God relates to you and your children?**

---

Instead of doing everything for them, love chooses
to let them learn what's involved in doing it
themselves. ... There should be nothing they can't
eventually do without our help. They must be fully
prepared to leave. —*The Love Dare for Parents*, day 38

---

We began this study by acknowledging that our masterpieces will not be with us forever.

**What additional steps will you commit to in order to redeem the time you still have and to better equip your children for the moment they leave home?**

Ultimately, God gave us children so we could introduce them to Him, showing them His love and His ways on earth. It is our hope that one day in eternity, He will introduce you to the many generations you blessed and helped lead into heaven. There we can see and enjoy His glory for all eternity.

> *My people, hear my instruction; listen to what I say.*
> *I will declare wise sayings; I will speak mysteries from the*
> *past—things we have heard and known and that our fathers*
> *have passed down to us. We must not hide them from their*
> *children, but must tell a future generation the praises of the*
> *LORD, His might, and the wonderful works He has performed.*
> *Psalm 78:1-4*

# RENEW

## GET SPECIFIC

1. **REFLECT** on the six weeks of your parenting walk. Ask and answer the following questions: What has meant the most to you during this study? What has God said to you personally as a result of the sessions? What three big action steps might you still need to take as a parent?

   To remind yourself of your goals and this experience, consider writing out and posting Psalm 78:1-8 in a location you will see frequently (above the kitchen sink, office computer, bathroom mirror). Read and pray over these verses.

2. **PRAY** that God would give you daily grace and wisdom to be a godly parent and example for your children. Then pray that God will mightily bless and use your children!

   Continue to pray daily for your children. Would you consider any to be prodigals? A disgruntled brother? Pray for all—that God would help them understand the beauty and nature of His undeserved grace.

3. **SURVEY** group members about actions they plan to take. There is something special about learning from and being motivated by one another (Heb. 10:24-25). Consider sharing progress through email or other methods of keeping in touch, so that accountability

and support continue. You never know whether one of your ideas might help another family in its Love Dare journey.

4. **DARE** to take action: "If one of your children is in a period of turmoil and confusion, write a short note to assure them of your consistent love, prayer, and support. Make a point to tell each of your kids that your love is a constant, no matter what. Ask if there's something you can help bear for them today." —*The Love Dare for Parents,* day 36

5. **OPTION**: Enriching this week's Bible study are days 36-40 of *The Love Dare for Parents: Love bears all things; Love fulfills dreams, Love liberates, Love never fails,* and *Love leaves a legacy.* (Also see pp. 86-87.)

---

Even when I am old and gray, God, do not abandon me.
Then I will proclaim Your power to another generation,
Your strength to all who are to come (Ps. 71:18).

---

# How to Find Peace with God

God created us to please and honor Him. But because of our pride and selfishness, every one of us has fallen short and dishonored God at different times in our lives. We have all sinned against Him, failing to bring Him the honor and glory He deserves from each of us (Rom. 3:23). This includes your children too.

God is holy, so He must reject all that is sinful (Matt. 13:41-43). Because He is perfect, He cannot allow our sin against Him to go unpunished, or else He would not be a just judge (Rom. 2:5-8). The Bible says that our sins separate us from God and that the "wages of sin is death" (Rom. 6:23). This death is not only physical but also spiritual, resulting in separation from God for eternity.

Out of His love and kindness for us, God sent His only Son, Jesus Christ, to die in our place and shed His blood to pay the price for our sins. Jesus' death satisfied the justice of God while providing a perfect demonstration of His mercy and love (Rom. 5:8; John 3:16). Three days later, God raised Him to life as our living Redeemer to prove that He is the Son of God (Rom. 1:4; Eph. 2:1-7).

He commands all people everywhere to repent and turn away from their sinful ways and humbly trust Jesus for their salvation. By surrendering your life to His lordship and control, you can have forgiveness and freely receive everlasting life (Rom. 10:9).

Is anything stopping you from surrendering your life to Jesus right now? If you understand your need to be forgiven and are ready to begin a relationship with God, we encourage you to pray now and trust your life to Jesus Christ. Be honest with God about your mistakes and your need for His forgiveness. Resolve to ask Him to help you turn from your sin and to place your trust in Him and in what He did on the cross. Then invite Him into your life to fill you, change your heart, and take control.

If you are not sure how to communicate your desires to Him, then use this prayer as a guide:

> Lord Jesus, I know I have sinned against You and deserve the judgment of God. I believe that You died on the cross to pay for my sins. I choose now to ask for Your forgiveness. Jesus, I'm making You the Lord and Boss of my life. Change me and help me now to live the rest of my life for You. Thank You for giving me a home in heaven with You when I die. Amen.

Here are some important next steps to take as a new Christian.

1. Find a Bible-teaching church and ask to be baptized as an expression of your new commitment in Him. Start attending on a regular basis, sharing life with other believers in Jesus Christ.

2. Locate a Bible you can understand and begin to read it for a few minutes every day. Start in the Gospel of John and work through the New Testament. Ask God to teach you how to love Him and walk with Him. Begin to talk with God in prayer—thanking Him for your new life, confessing your sins when you fail, and asking for what you need.

3. Take advantage of the opportunities God gives you to share your faith with others. There is no greater joy than to know God and to make Him known!

4. If you have received God's forgiveness for your sins through faith and by His grace—whether now or many years ago—share this wonderful news with your family and children.

Adapted from Appendix V, "How to find peace with God,"
*The Love Dare for Parents* (Nashville, B&H Publishing).

# Leader Notes

Many parents in your community have likely seen a Sherwood Pictures movie (FLYWHEEL, FACING THE GIANTS, FIREPROOF, or COURAGEOUS) or attended a Bible study by Alex and Stephen Kendrick. Consequently, this may be a good study to promote beyond your church. Allow sufficient advance promotion time and use your church website, social media, and other means to get the word out. Don't assume everyone knows how to get to the study site, so provide clear directions and a contact number.

Choose a setting that works best for the parents you are trying to reach; multiple groups may be an option. Work to make your group a welcoming place. Keep in mind guests to your church, single parents, or parents attending without his or her spouse.

Six group sessions allow participants to establish relationships with other parents. Explain the importance of continuing accountability once the group is over. Lead the group to use the activities and questions to discuss the content for each session. **RENEW** activities are designed to be done between sessions but can be done as a group if preferred. Before dismissing each week, draw attention to the **RENEW** applications.

Ideally, you will use *The Love Dare for Parents* to enhance the group experience. Doing so may encourage some in your group to add this resource to their Bible study. Those who are not able to read and do all the daily love dares will still benefit as you share insights and information.

You may want to email your group during the week. Encourage folk to use the Group Directory (p. 96) to keep in touch.

One benefit of a small group is to find and build leaders. Be on the lookout for church members who might facilitate future small-group studies.

**SESSION 1:** Always review key Scriptures for each session. Also look over "Group Guidelines" (pp. 7-8) and allow the group to adjust as needed. Encourage participants to sign the pact, indicating their commitment to the group, to God, and to their families.

It could be easy to spend too much time on how frazzled parents are. Some are, but many are not. Get acquainted but move promptly into biblical solutions. Be a good steward of everyone's time by keeping the session on target. Always close in prayer.

**SESSION 2:** Be sensitive to any parent who may not be a Christian. Remain to talk with parents about questions or how to share Christ with their children. Review "How to Find Peace with God" (pp. 82-83) as you prepare.

**SESSION 3:** Be ready to talk about boundaries and how they helped you growing up. Parents' responsibility to confront sin in their children's lives may be hard for some to grasp. Pray for God's leading in a special way for this session.

**SESSION 4:** Briefly play "Simon Says" to get this point across quickly: example speaks louder than words. Parents model godly faith, relationships, and marriage.

**SESSION 5:** Research David's life to help the group process "The Good, the Bad, the Ugly" activity (1 Sam. 16–2 Sam.). Think through challenges parents face in today's culture, and help parents see how appropriate conversations can be taking place with children of all ages.

**SESSION 6:** God's love anchors this study, as launching children well concludes the group sessions. In some way acknowledge the significant achievement parents have made by participating. Pray for God to provide daily grace and wisdom for group members to be godly examples for their children—and that God will mightily bless and use the children represented by this group!

# Daily Love Dares Overview

### Session 1: SACRED TRUST

| Day | Summary |
|---|---|
| 1. Love blooms | Create a home in which children can flourish. |
| 2. Love is patient | Be slow to anger. Don't provoke your children to wrath (Eph. 6:4). |
| 3. Love is kind | Be engaged and intentional. Reach out. Meet needs. |
| 4. Love values | Children are a blessing, inheritance, fruit, and reward, not a curse. |
| 5. Love is wonderful | God created your children unique. Relate to and train them appropriately. |
| 6. Love is not selfish | Truly loving requires self denial. Dedicate kids to God! |
| 7. Love is not irritable | Love is not easily provoked. |

### Session 2: SPECIFIC MASTERPIECE

| | |
|---|---|
| 8. Love wins hearts | Win and keep your children's hearts. |
| 9. Love cherishes | Love is affectionate. |
| 10. Love is not rude | Mind your manners and teach manners to your children. |
| 11. Love teaches | Teach 24/7 life lessons and skills. |
| 12. Love encourages | Value your kids with words and actions. |
| 13. Love disciplines | Explain the what, how, and why of correction. |
| 14. Love is compassionate | Love provides safety. |
| 15. Love is from God | God is the source of true love. |

### Session 3: SECURE BOUNDARIES

| | |
|---|---|
| 16. Love respects God | Teach children the fear of the Lord. |
| 17. Love seeks God's blessing | Your faith, obedience, and integrity matter. |
| 18. Love models the way | Love children through a strong marriage. |
| 19. Love protects | Protect physically, emotionally, and spiritually. Teach discernment. |

20. **Love takes time**    Give quality time. Say no to secondary things.
21. **Love is fair**    Don't set kids up to be jealous of one another.

## Session 4: SERIOUS RESPONSIBILITY

22. **Love honors authority**  Teach children to honor all authority.
23. **Love intercedes**    Pray and help kids fight spiritual battles.
24. **Love forgives**    Forgive your children, your spouse, and your own parents.
25. **Love takes responsibility**    Love asks for forgiveness. Confession is powerful.
26. **Love is Jesus Christ**    Jesus loves you and your kids. Lead your kids to Christ.
27. **Love is satisfied in God**  Walk with God and abide intimately.
28. **Love is God's Word**    Let God's Word guide your parenting. Get children into it.

## Session 5: SHARED PATH

29. **Love listens**    Pursue understanding. Ask questions.
30. **Love shepherds hearts**  Help children process life experiences.
31. **Love influences**    Provide multiple godly influences.
32. **Love prepares**    Initiate discussions related to seasons of life.
33. **Love blesses**    Cast a vision; water God's seeds; set up success.
34. **Love and marriage**    Help your kids guard purity and eventually marry well.
35. **Love rejoices in truth**  Love confronts evil and speaks truth.

## Session 6: STEADFAST COMMITMENT

36. **Love bears all things**    When kids blow it, help them turn things around. Pray daily.
37. **Love fulfills dreams**    Help kids meet heroes and accomplish goals.
38. **Love liberates**    Launch kids into life and ultimately let go.
39. **Love never fails**    Parental influence never stops. Don't give up on your children.
40. **Love leaves a legacy**    Leave a legacy of wealth, wisdom, love, faith, and example.

# How to Pray for Your Children

*Not only does God promise to reward the person who prays persistently with believing faith (Matt. 7:7-8), the habit of praying for each member of your family will draw you closer (2 Thess. 1:11).*

*Pray that they will:*

1. Love the Lord their God with all their heart, soul, mind, and strength, and their neighbors as themselves (Matt. 22:36-38).

2. Come to know Christ as Lord early in life (2 Tim. 3:15).

3. Develop a hatred for evil and sin (Ps. 97:10; 38:18; Prov. 8:13).

4. Be protected from evil spiritually, emotionally, mentally, and physically (John 17:15; 10:10; Rom. 12:9).

5. Be caught when they are guilty and receive the chastening of the Lord (Ps. 119:71; Heb. 12:5-6).

6. Receive wisdom, understanding, knowledge, and discretion from the Lord (Dan. 1:17,20; Prov. 1:4; Jas. 1:5).

7. Respect and submit to authority (Rom. 13:1; Eph. 6:1-3; Heb. 13:17).

8. Be surrounded by the right kinds of friends and avoid wrong friends (Prov. 1:10-16; 13:20).

9. Find a godly mate and raise godly children who will live for Christ (2 Cor. 6:14-17; Deut. 6).

10. Walk in sexual and moral purity (1 Cor. 6:18-20).

11. Keep a clear conscience that remains tender before the Lord (Acts 24:16; 1 Tim. 1:19; 4:1-2; Titus 1:15-16).

12. Not fear any evil but walk in the fear of the Lord (Ps. 23:4; Deut. 10:12).

13. Be a blessing to your family, the church, and the cause of Christ in the world (Matt. 28:18-20; Eph. 1:3; 4:29).

14. Be filled with the knowledge of God's will and fruitful in every good work (Eph. 1:16-19; Phil. 1:11; Col. 1:9).

15. Overflow with love, discern what is best, and be blameless until the day of Christ (Phil. 1:9-10).

Adapted from Appendix III, "How to pray for your children,"
*The Love Dare for Parents* (Nashville, B&H Publishing).

# The Word of God in Your Life

*Let this proclamation help parents to rightly approach God's Word.*
The Bible is the Word of God.

It is holy, inerrant, infallible, and completely authoritative (Prov. 30:5-6; John 17:17; Ps. 119:89).

It is profitable for teaching, reproving, correcting, and training me in righteousness (2 Tim. 3:16).

It matures and equips me to be ready for every good work (2 Tim. 3:17).

It is a lamp to my feet and a light to my path (Ps. 119:105).

It makes me wiser than my enemies (Ps. 119:97-100).

It brings me stability during the storms of my life (Matt. 7:24-27).

If I believe its truth, I will be set free (John 8:32).

If I hide it in my heart, I will be protected in times of temptation (Ps. 119:11).

If I continue in it, I will become a true disciple (John 8:31).

If I meditate on it, I will become successful (Josh. 1:8).

If I keep it, I will be rewarded and my love perfected
(Ps. 19:7-11; 1 John 2:5).

It is the living, powerful, discerning Word of God
(Heb. 4:12).

It is the sword of the Spirit (Eph. 6:17).

It is sweeter than honey and more desirable than gold
(Ps. 19:10).

It is indestructible and forever settled in heaven
(Ps. 119:89).

It is absolutely true with no mixture of error
(John 17:17; Titus 1:2).

It is absolutely true about God (Rom. 3:4; 16:25; Col. 1).

It is absolutely true about man (Jer. 17:9; Ps. 8:4-6).

It is absolutely true about sin (Rom. 3:23).

It is absolutely true about salvation (Acts 4:12;
Rom. 10:9).

It is absolutely true about heaven and hell (Rev. 21:8).

Adapted from Appendix VIII, "The Word of God in my life,"
*The Love Dare for Parents* (Nashville, B&H Publishing).

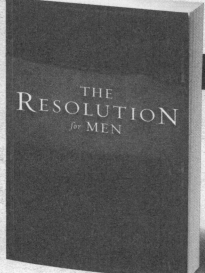

The next step after the movie *Courageous*, *The Resolution for Men* by **Stephen** and **Alex Kendrick** with **Randy Alcorn**, is an inspiring call and clear guide helping men to take full physical, social, and spiritual responsibility as fathers and husbands.

## BASED ON THE FILM COURAGEOUS
# *Live the Resolution*

From best-selling author **Priscilla Shirer**, a call for women to live intentionally to honor God and their families.

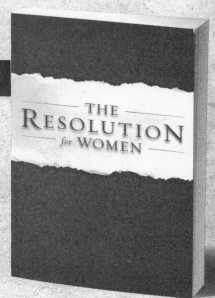

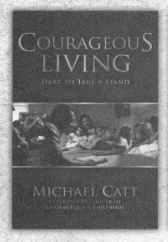

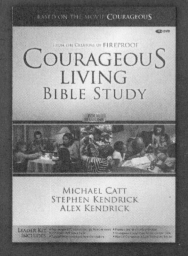

# Group Directory

*You can pray more intentionally when you get to know your fellow group members. Include this information to stay better connected.*

| Name | Email/Phone Number | Family Information |
|------|-------------------|-------------------|
| 1. | | |
| 2. | | |
| 3. | | |
| 4. | | |
| 5. | | |
| 6. | | |
| 7. | | |
| 8. | | |
| 9. | | |
| 10. | | |
| 11. | | |
| 12. | | |